I Want
A Pet
Lowchen

Gail Forsyth

This publication has been researched and designed to provide accurate pet care, while helping children learn the responsibilities that entail having to care for their Lowchen.

No part of this book is to be copied without written permission from the publisher and author.

Breed Profiles Publishing
Cedar City, UT 84721

All rights reserved. © 2014

Table of Contents

Note To Parents From The Author	1
Acknowledgment	2
My Pledge	3
Personal Page	4
Always Wash Your Hands	5
General Information on Dogs	6
Traits and Characteristics	9
Door Hanger	10
Questions and Answers	12
Word Find	13
History of Dogs	14
Dogs by Group	15
Missing Vowels	16
Word Find	17
Words to Unscramble	18
Questions and Answers on Origin	19
First Day at Home	20
My Bed and Crate	22
Housebreaking	24
Healthy Foods For Puppies	26
What Not To Feed Your Puppy	27
Vitamins & Minerals	28
Questions and Answers on Food	29
Wheat-Free Dog Treats	30
Treat Canister	31
Teething and Chewing	33
Spay and Neuter	34
Grooming	35
Bugs	38
Color Me	39
Toys	40
Collar and Leash	41
Chain Collar	42
Training Chart	43
Collars	44
Obedience Training	46
Teaching The Come Command	47
Teaching The Heel Command	49
Teaching The Sit Command	51
Teaching The Stay Command	52
Teaching The Lie Down Command	54

Teaching The Stand Command	56
Questions and Answers on Training	57
Missing Vowels	58
Unscramble These Training Words	59
Word Find Puzzle on Training	60
Barking	61
Traveling	62
Color Me	63
Counting Paws	64
Health Issues	65
Water Hazards	67
Missing Vowels	68
Word Find	69
Is Your Dog A Blue Ribbon Winner	70
Daily Care Chart	71
Identification	72
Unscramble These Words	73
Taking Me Outdoors	74
Tails	75
Ears	77
Paw Print Paper Weight	78
Make Your Own Note Cards	79
Make Your Own Bookmarks	82
Puppy Maze	84
Fun and Games	85
Missing Vowels	89
Unscramble These Words	90
Happy Birthday Card	91
Draw Me	94
More Dog Books	95

Note To Parents From The Author

As a parent and grandparent myself, I know the cries and wants of a child that desires a pet. When I was a child I had the same wishes to obtain just about every kind of pet I could. Every book I bought or checked out at the library was pet or animal related.

If your child has been asking for a Lowchen, only you know if he or she is ready to take on that commitment.

Your supervision will ensure that the dog is being well cared for and you'll be pleased with watching your child learn to care and nurture a pet. They may even grow up to follow a career in the pet field.

Puppies or dogs can be a good choice for older children. However, they do require more care and training than many other types of pets.

You'll find this book will help your child learn about the needs of their dog and all the while having a fun time doing it. The book has basic care topics that your child can read, plus interactive games, mazes, questions and answers, and care charts.

Childhood lasts such a short time, but the memories with a pet will last a lifetime.

Acknowledgment

I would like to acknowledge my family for all their help and words of encouragement while taking the idea for the books all the way to getting them published.

To my mother, who certainly endured some trying years when I would bring home every animal I could get my hands on.

To my children, who are a great inspiration in so much of who I am, and whose father inspired them into becoming the fine adults they are today.

To my husband, for his endless patience on the time I've spent with my own pets. However, it is not true that the pets eat better than he does! Honest.

A great big "Thank You" to each and every one of you.

Gail Forsyth

My Pledge

Being a responsible pet owner, I understand that it takes daily care to be sure that my dog gets the care it deserves.

I pledge to feed my dog everyday.

I pledge to never abuse my dog. I will never hit my dog.

I pledge to give my dog fresh water everyday.

I pledge to keep my dog clean and well groomed.

I pledge to train my dog so that it becomes smart and trustworthy.

I pledge to play with my dog everyday.

I pledge to give my dog a warm and dry spot to sleep.

I pledge to read books on dogs, if I need to find out something about their care and training.

I pledge to always wash my hands after playing or cleaning up after my dog.

Signed,   Date:

_____   _____

Personal Page For Your Lowchen

Your Name _____

Your Age _____

Name of Your Lowchen _____

Date Born _____

Color of Your Lowchen _____

Date Obtained _____

Obtained From _____

Veterinarian _____

Paste a Picture of You and Your

Lowchen Here

**Always Wash Your Hands After Feeding or Cleaning Up After Your Dog.
Draw Some Colorful Bubbles!**

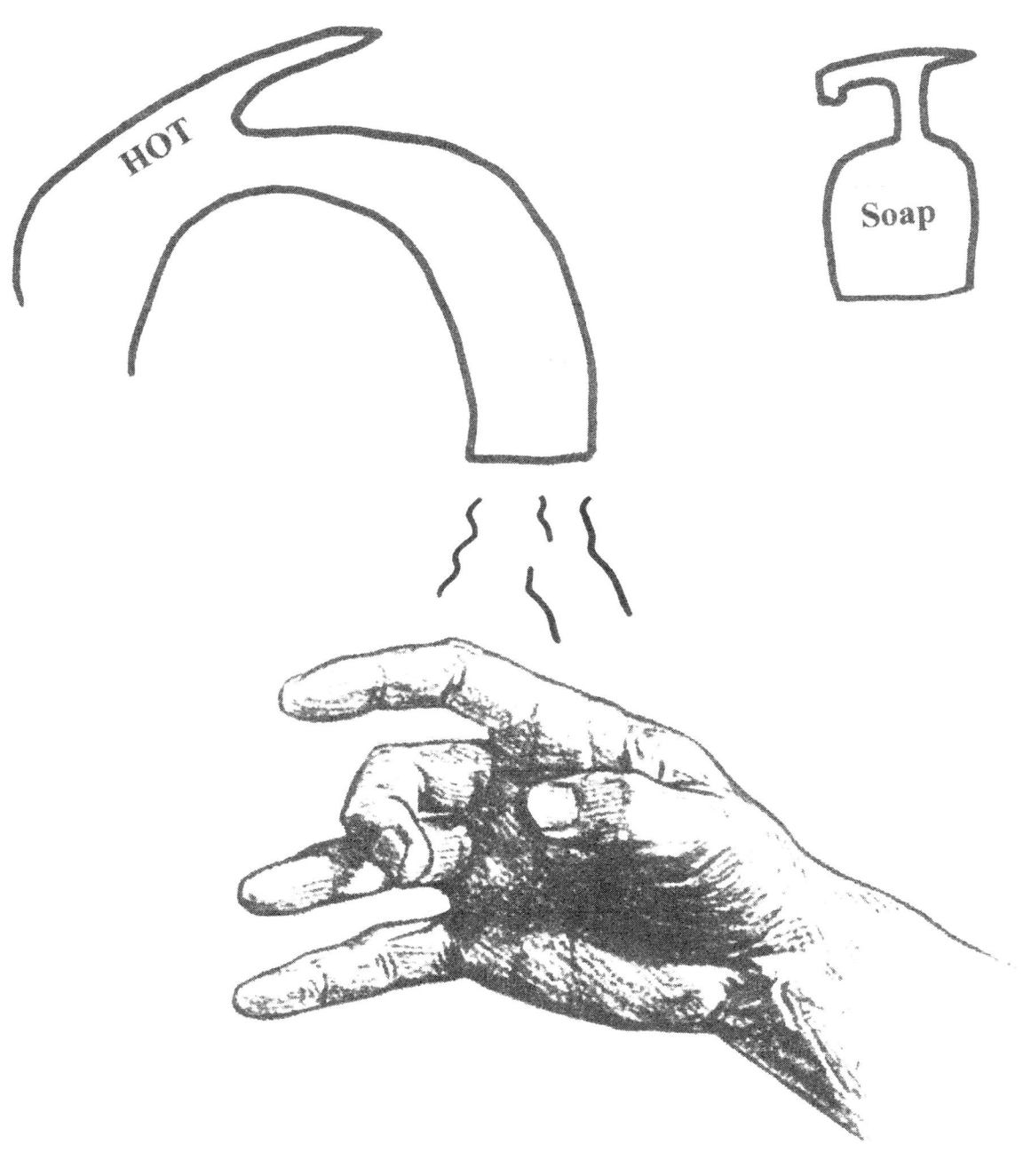

General Information on Dogs

So you've been wanting a Lowchen for a pet. You've promised to take care of it, feed it and clean up after it. You think a Lowchen would be fun to have as a pet. Well, I am a Lowchen and my name is Sugar.

It takes more than just playing, holding and admiring my good looks to give me the proper care that I need. I'll tell you a little bit about what I like and what you'll need to do to make me happy and keep me healthy.

Ask yourself if my traits and characteristics fit your lifestyle.

Are you active and do you like to go on hikes, walks or ride your bike? Or do you prefer to stay indoors and watch television or play video games?

Dogs need to have exercise every day. Are you willing to groom me and keep me looking good?

I need fresh water and a good quality dog food to eat, everyday.

All dogs need training too. So you'll need to set some time aside each and everyday to be sure that I not only learn the basic commands that every dog should learn, but also on how to behave around people and other pets.

All in all, I am fairly easy to care for. Just remember that all my care will fall on your shoulders. I can't get my own food, my own water or adjust the temperature to keep me comfortable. My care will have to last my whole life, each and everyday, not just for a few weeks. Are you willing to do this for me? If your answer is yes, then this book will help you to learn how to take care of me.

Here is some general information on puppies and dogs. We'll discuss some of these topics in further detail in the book.

Well, you know that I am also called a canine.

Dogs are meat eaters.

We will sometimes eat things that we shouldn't.

I am a clean creature and I like a clean home.

Do you know where I will be sleeping at night? Discuss this with your family so we can start off with the correct sleeping arrangements. It is better to have me sleep in one spot, rather than move me around from place to place. This can get confusing to me.

I am not too hard to train, patience and kindness is key.

Training is important for me to grow up and to be a good dog.

I require a clean home to stay healthy.

Taking me to a veterinarian for proper shots and worming is important for my health.

I can get parasites, such as mites, ticks, fleas and worms.

I am a social creature and I like to interact with humans and other pets that I have learned to enjoy and play with.

When you first get me and take me home, go slow with me and don't make any fast movements or loud noises when you are near me. Let me get to know you. I must learn to trust you and know that you will not harm me. The world is a big place and all this is new to me. There are so many new things to sniff and explore. Don't rush me. Before long I'll learn the routine that you have set up for me and we'll be best friends with years to enjoy each other and to learn from each other.

If you pick me up be sure to hold me securely so I don't fall. I may be a little jumpy at first, so sit close to the ground just in case I get away from you, I won't have too far to fall.

If you pick me up don't swing me in circles or throw me up in the air. Never, ever hit me. If you hit me, this will make me afraid of you and I will try to run away when you are near me. Even a slight tap can hurt me or injure me and could even cause me to die.

I do like to explore. When you allow me this freedom be sure to keep me away from electrical cords, appliances and other objects that could cause me harm. Keep me away from the fireplace or stove if they are on, I might get too close and get burned.

Be careful not to step on me. I am faster than you think. If you need to do other things and can't watch me while I explore, put me back in my pen or crate for my own safety, until I know the rules of the house. Only take me out when you are able to keep an eye on me the whole time. This helps with my housebreaking too. Don't just let me wander about the house without your supervision. I may use the restroom anyplace and anytime.

Puppies do very well if confined to a pen or crate during the early stages of housebreaking and learning about what I can or can't do, things I can touch or places I can explore within the house.

Watch me and be sure I don't tumble down any stairs. Teach me how to go up and down the stairs safely.

Some dogs and cats will accept me into the household. They may just give me a sniff and pay me no attention or will want to play. Don't trust any dogs or cats around me if they are not being supervised. Some dogs and cats can get territorial with their home and may not like me coming into the home that they have called their own. Give us all time to become buddies.

While I am out of my pen exploring be extra cautious that nobody opens the door that leads out of the house. I might just slip on outside. You can hang a little sign on the door that says that I "am loose", to warn them that I am out of my pen and exploring. The next page has a handy door hanger for you to write my name on, color and cut it out and hang on the door. Decorate the backside of the door hanger too.

Traits and Characteristics

The Lowchen originated in Europe.

As with most breeds, the exact heritage of a dog can be blurred by the years, in that countries change names and dogs were transferred and given as gifts from one person in one country to another person in another country. You can learn about many of these differences by reading dog books.

It was used primarily as a foot warmer for women.

The Lowchen belongs to the Non-Sporting group, in the AKC registry.

The Lowchen measures 10 - 13 inches tall at the shoulders. The males tend to be bigger than the females.

They can weigh in at 9 to 18 pounds when full grown.

The fur on a Lowchen comes in white, black and lemon, or speckled.

The fur is long and soft. Usually cut in the typical "lion look".

The Lowchen is very intelligent and loyal. They are playful, alert, and affectionate. They would make a good pet for an active family, and they generally enjoy people.

Draw a Lowchen Below.

Door Hanger

Write your dog's name on the line below. Then color this door hanger, cut it out and hang it on the door when I am allowed to have some free time to explore.

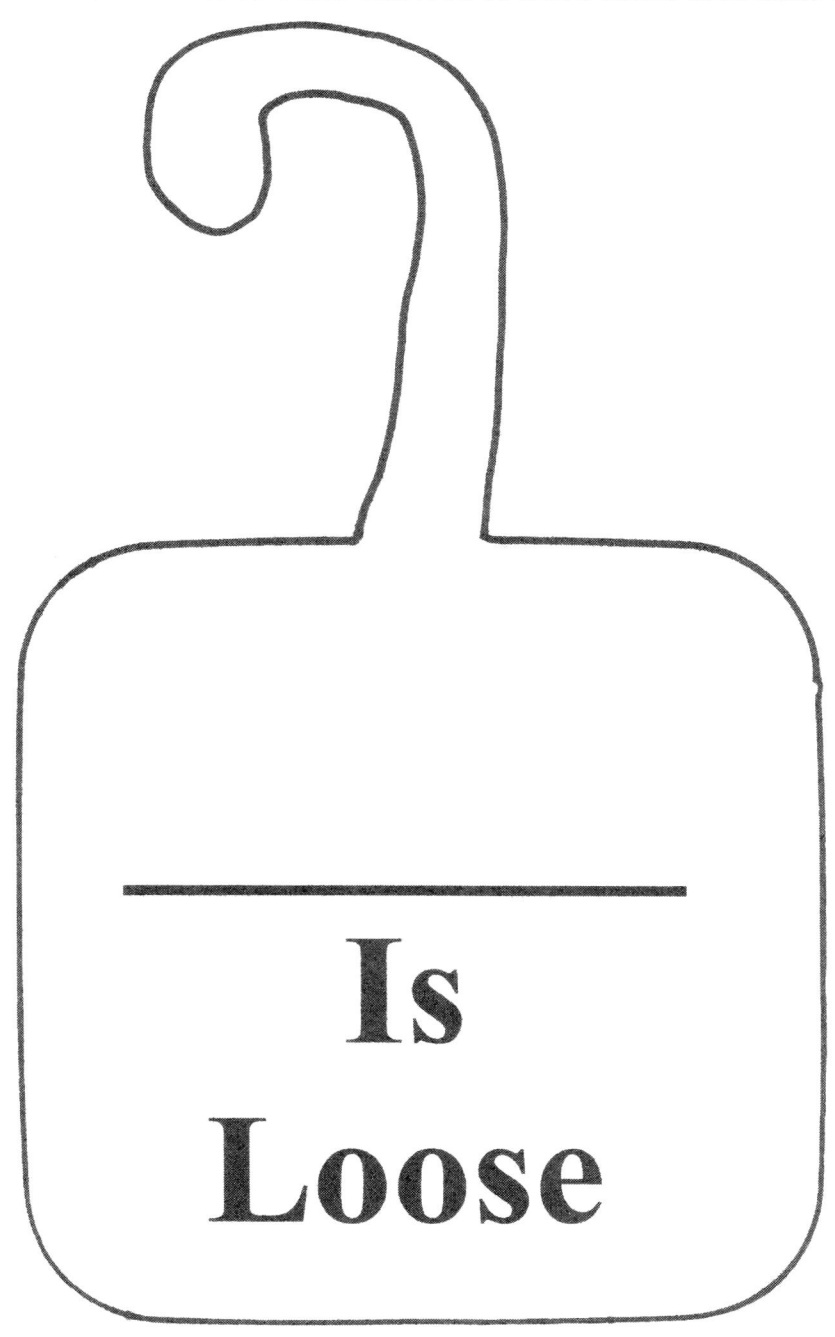

Make a Backside of the Door Hanger

Questions and Answers

Here are six questions for you to answer on my basic housing and care.

Am I easy to train? _____

Do I need shots? _____

Am I a meat eater or a plant eater? _____

Do I need shade from the sun? _____

Will I rely on you for all my care? _____

Am I a social creature? _____

I hope you got all the answers correct.

Word Find

Below is a word find puzzle. Can you find the following words in the puzzle? Circle the words and check them off the list when you find them.

___ PUPPY

___ FOOD

___ WATER

___ TAIL

___ SLEEP

___ PLANTS

___ HIDE

___ SHADE

___ WARMTH

___ TREATS

___ COLOR

___ PAWS

B	N	D	V	F	O	O	D	R	P	F	A	S	M	P	A	W	S	G	Z
M	H	S	L	E	E	P	I	T	S	B	F	U	R	A	W	A	T	E	R
U	S	A	A	G	H	J	U	M	P	E	E	N	C	T	P	M	S	A	P
C	H	I	D	E	E	T	R	U	P	V	A	S	S	T	L	W	A	T	L
P	E	M	P	P	L	E	M	H	O	V	S	H	A	D	E	E	H	O	A
U	D	O	X	I	O	P	R	R	A	C	C	I	A	S	R	J	H	N	N
P	A	N	S	J	E	R	T	Y	U	B	I	N	N	Y	B	A	B	G	T
P	H	O	P	V	B	V	C	A	E	A	S	E	R	S	U	N	N	U	S
Y	I	T	N	T	G	H	K	A	C	A	R	R	B	Y	W	R	X	E	O
A	J	U	P	P	C	O	L	O	R	U	W	A	T	A	I	L	S	I	N
K	W	A	R	M	T	H	B	E	C	C	O	T	R	E	A	T	S	L	N

History of Dogs

So how did I become man's best friend? Dogs as we know them today, evolved over the years from wolves. Years ago, wolves and man had crossed paths. As wolves stayed close to man and his home, they would scavenge for left over food and bones that was at the man's camp.

Over the years wolf pups were brought back home to the man's camp. These pups grew up around man and helped him hunt for food and to protect him and his family from other predators.

In return, man would provide shelter, warmth from the camp fire and food to the wolf pups as they grew. This created a strong bond between man and the wolves.

In time, the wolves had become quite tame. They also had begun to change with the climate and the terrain in which they lived. Man started to breed the now domesticated wolves to suit man's needs. In cold climates, they bred wolves to have heavier coats. Some were bred to be very agile to get over rocks and rough terrain in pursuit of the game that they would chase down to eat. Some were bred to be small to chase vermin down holes and to rid the home of these disease ridden pests.

Man even started to use these wolves to help them tend their livestock and to keep predators from harming the livestock. These wolves became very useful to man.

None of this happened overnight. This took thousands of years. So the relationship with dogs and humans goes back along way.

Wolves are very social creatures, as are our dogs. Our dogs of today prefer human companionship, rather than being alone.

Today, dogs are trained for all sorts of work and pleasure. It is no wonder that we have developed into "man's best friend".

Dogs by Group

Purebred dogs are classified into different categories called "groups".

These groups pertain to what the dog was bred for. New breeds of dogs are often put in the miscellaneous group.

The groups are listed below:

Sporting Group

Working Group

Toy Group

Terrier Group

Herding Group

Hound Group

Non-Sporting Group

Miscellaneous Group

What group does your dog fall into? _____

Missing Vowels

Below are words that need a vowel. These words can all be found in the chapters on the History of Dogs and Traits and Characteristics.

Use these vowels   A – E – I – O – U – Y

C _ _ N T R _

_ R _ G _ N

F _ R

W _ L V _ S

F R _ _ N D

P R _ T _ C T

S _ C _ _ L

G R _ _ P

C _ L _ R S

S _ Z _

G R _ _ M _ N G

W _ _ G H T

W _ R L D

_ R _ G _ N _ T _

G R _ W N

Word Find

Below is a word find puzzle. These words pertain to dogs. Circle the words in the puzzle and cross them off your list.

CANINE

PAWS

FUR

GROOM

TRAIN

EARS

BARK

GROWL

TAIL

T	A	I	L	C	A	Q	W	E	R	Y	T	O	M
F	I	R	C	B	A	R	K	C	A	N	I	N	B
C	H	I	V	B	G	R	O	W	L	Y	T	U	R
F	U	X	P	U	L	B	O	O	M	E	Q	W	S
V	J	J	I	M	V	H	U	R	P	A	W	S	O
X	E	A	R	S	Z	E	E	T	T	R	A	I	M
V	B	H	H	R	Y	T	R	A	I	N	X	M	W
P	O	O	F	H	E	K	L	C	A	N	I	N	E
B	F	U	R	T	U	J	O	I	B	N	M	A	Q
R	U	T	T	G	R	O	O	M	M	G	T	E	A

Words to Unscramble

Below are some letters to unscramble and make them into words.
These words can all be found in the previous chapters.

CNOUTYR

NORIIG

TSTAIR

PGRUO

URF

WOVLSE

HNUT

OVNIERGHT

LISCOA

SHPICOMANPNOI

TECTPRO

DGOS

WAPS

FULUSE

YREAS

THSANDOUS

Questions and Answers on Origin

Dogs have originated from different parts of the world and were bred for specific duties. Below are some questions about me. You'll find the correct answers in the previous chapters.

What country did I originate from? _____

What was I originally used for? _____

What group of dogs do I belong to? _____

How tall will I be when I am full grown? _____

What colors do I come in? _____

What is my ideal weight when I am full grown? _____

What type of fur do I have? _____

First Day at Home

Oh what an exciting day this is. You and me together at last.

This is a happy time for both of us, I can feel your excitement.

I don't really know what is going on. All these strange sounds and smells. Everyone seems so joyful. But I'm still a little scared.

It would be best to slow down and let me get accustomed to you and others in your family and household.

I'm sure you'll want to show me off to all your friends. There will be time for that after I get settled in. Don't overwhelm me with too much to see and do. There is so much going on. I need my rest. Too much playing and activity can make me ill or upset.

Let me wander around from person to person. Don't chase me around. Don't make loud noises around me or move too fast. This will scare me.

Set up my sleeping area for me.

Show me where my food and water bowls are.

Don't feed me too much and don't feed me people food. This could upset my tender tummy.

This is a big day for you and me. This will be the start of us becoming the very best of friends.

We'll be able to do more and more each day, as I get used to your schedule and all the people and any other animals that live in the same house.

Puppies and dogs are very curious as to their surroundings. You will notice that I want to investigate everything and every inch of my new home. This is okay for me to do. Just keep a close eye on me so that I don't get into any trouble.

Close off any rooms that you don't want me to wander into.

Don't let me wander in the garage. There are way too many things that are not good for me in there. If any anti-freeze has dripped onto the garage floor and I take a lick of it, this can be deadly to me.

Don't put me outside without supervision. I might chew on the plants or start to dig holes or I could even get lost or stolen. If the weather is snowy or wet be sure to dry me off when you bring me back indoors.

As a puppy, I will need to sleep often. This is a good time for you to sit with me and read a book out loud. I'll love the sound of your voice and it can be reassuring to me as I fall asleep.

I hope that you have all of my necessary supplies. As the days go by you may decide that you need something else for me from the pet supply store. If I have had my puppy shots, I would love to go to the pet store and get whatever else you need for me, and maybe even a little treat. If I have not had my puppy shots, it would be best if I stay home until the puppy shots have all been given to me.

Keeping me safe and healthy will mean that I can't go where other dogs and puppies are until I've had my shots.

This may be a good time for you to schedule my next appointment with the veterinarian to keep my shots up to date and for me to get to know him or her.

My Bed and Crate

Having a place of my own to sleep is important. It will make me feel at home and make me feel safe.

A crate is a safe place for me. There may be times when you will want to close the door on my crate so that I don't come out.

If I haven't been accustomed to a crate before you brought me home, you will need to teach me that a crate is a good place for me and that I am to lay quietly when I am in there.

You can teach me this very easily. Put a nice soft towel in the crate for me to lie down on. Put me in the crate with one of my favorite toys and maybe a small treat or something to chew on. Give me a command such as, "go to sleep" or "where's your bed?" Do this after we have been playing hard or taken a long walk. Then I'll be ready for a nap. You can sit down next to me and read a book or take a nap yourself. Knowing that you are close by will comfort me. Especially in the beginning when I am learning about the crate. Don't put my crate in a busy, noisy part of the house. It sometimes helps to cover my crate with a blanket to make it a little darker. This will help me sleep.

Put me in my crate periodically during the day. If I whine and cry, don't let me out. If you let me out, that will only teach me that whining and crying will get me out of the crate. This is not what you want. Only let me out once I've been quiet for a time, or after I've woken up from my nap.

Puppies and dogs like a place of their own. Having them sleep in their own bed is safer for them too. If you let them sleep on your bed with you, they might fall off and hurt themselves, or you could roll over on them and hurt them, and they could even use your bed as a bathroom.

Don't confuse me by letting me sleep on your bed one night and then putting me into my crate on another night. Have me sleep in my crate from day one of you bringing me home. If you are lucky and I've already been crate trained and are used to sleeping in one, your nights will go a lot smoother. If not, then this will be a part of the training that I need.

Having your puppy in a crate at night when you are sleeping will prevent your puppy from wandering around the house and getting into things that are unsafe.

The crate will also help to housebreak your puppy. You'll read more on how to do this in another chapter.

Crates are also wonderful and safe for me when I am riding in the car. If I am safely in my crate, I won't be able to slip out of a car door or fall out of a car window. The crate will also prevent me from jumping from seat to seat and distracting the driver of the vehicle.

Once I am grown up and have learned the rules of the house and have become housebroken and know where to use the restroom, you can safely leave the door to my crate open and let me come and go as I need.

Crate training is easy to do, but it does take time.

Remember that even though your puppy may cry while he is in the crate at first, he is not being hurt. Like any training, your puppy just needs time to adjust and realize that you are in charge of his safety and well being.

Housebreaking

Housebreaking a puppy takes time, repetition and patience.

First off, never rub your puppies nose in any accidents that has happened in the house. This is disgusting and may actually cause me to not care if I am clean.

Being a clean creature will help in my wanting to stay clean and not soil my bed or crate.

It is important to remember that puppies need to go to the bathroom often.

Depending on your living arrangements, you may want me to go outside to use the restroom. Some people may want me to use potty pads or even a litter box. Decide this now, so you don't confuse me.

If you can, establish a routine for me by taking me outside or to my potty pads, about every 3 to 4 hours. Take me there after I wake up, after I eat and after I've been playing. Take me there one last time before we settle in for the night. Take note of my habits.

Each time I use the restroom in the right spot, praise me and tell me how smart I am.

Don't yell at me or hit me if I have an accident. Just clean up the mess and try to get me to my potty area a little sooner. As I grow, I'll be able to go longer between potty visits.

Having me on a regular feeding schedule will help too.

Using a crate makes this so much easier. Don't give me run of the house. When you can not watch me, put me back in my crate. This is not cruel. Dogs like the feeling of a cozy den. When you bring me back out of the crate, take me immediately to my potty area. Give me a command such as, "go potty" or "hurry up." Stay with me so that you can see if I used the restroom. If I did, praise me! Now you can give me a little more freedom in the house. But not for too long, and don't take your eyes off of me, as I'll need to use the restroom again before too long.

Don't expect miracles here. I am just a puppy. It will take me some time to understand what you are trying to get me to do.

By using and confining me to a crate, you'll notice that I really like to try to keep my living area clean. As I get older, my control will get much better.

If I do have an accident in my crate, they are very easy to clean. Don't yell at me for having an accident. I really do want to learn, but yelling will make me scared.

Don't go into a long speech about what I am suppose to do. I will not be able to understand what you are saying. Instead, keep me on a schedule for my eating times, playtimes and naps. Give me just a simple command when you take me to my potty area and praise me when I go.

Before long, I'll be housebroken and you'll be able to trust me to have free reign in the house.

Healthy Foods For Puppies

Keeping me healthy and happy with a proper diet is not too hard to do.

There are a lot of different foods at the pet store for you to choose from.

Some of these foods are made especially for puppies, and some are for grown dogs. You'll see both dry kibble in a bag or box along with a huge assortment of canned foods.

Ask the person who you are getting me from what food I have been eating. Then continue with this same food when you take me home. Any sudden changes of food can cause me to vomit or get diarrhea. If you want to change my food to another brand, do it over a period of about a week. Just add a little of the new food that you want me to eat, to the old food and give me a little less of my old food.

Do not switch my food around. Try to keep me on the same diet, especially while I am young and growing.

Dogs were made to eat meat. Having this meat in a complete and balanced dog food is the easiest way for me to get all the vitamins and minerals that I need. Trying to make a home made dog food is very difficult to get all the proper ingredients together to make the food healthy.

Feed me as close to the same time each day or night. Depending on my age I may need four small meals a day while I am young. As an adult you can either feed me one meal or two meals per day, plus a snack every once in a while.

When giving me treats when you are training me, offer me small nutritious pieces so I don't ruin my appetite for my main meal.

I know that I have the most cutest face in the world when I am begging for food, but try to avoid giving me too much people food. By getting too much people food I can become a picky eater and won't want the dog food that is so much better for me.

What Not To Feed Your Puppy

Here is a list of things that I should not eat. Please take care of me and don't feed me these foods or plants. Many will make me ill and possibly kill me.

Oleander
Chocolate
Soda Pop
Poinsettia
Mistletoe
Caffeine
Candy
Alcohol
Raisins
Chicken bones

Many house plants and outdoor plants are not good for me to chew on. Some of these can be poisonous. Keep me away from these, and teach me to leave them alone.

Vitamins & Minerals

If you are feeding me a good well-balanced diet, I may not need any extra vitamins and minerals unless I have been sick for some reason.

If I have been ill, your veterinarian will instruct you on how to give me any extra vitamins or minerals to make me better.

Never feed me your vitamins. Those are for people and they could make me very sick.

Watch me so that I don't take any medicines or vitamins that are left out on a table or counter.

Questions and Answers on Food

Here are a few questions for you to answer on what foods to feed me and what foods I should not eat.

What foods will make up my main diet? _____

Can I eat candy? _____

Can I eat raisins? _____

Should I have soda pop? _____

Chocolate sure smells good. Can I eat chocolate? _____

Can you name a plant that is not good for me? _____

I hope you got these questions correct.

Food is an important part of my day. Eating the correct foods will keep me happy and healthy. I know you are in charge of feeding me correctly.

Wheat-Free Dog Treats

Have a grown-up help you with making these tasty dog treats.

1 cup oatmeal
1 cup rye flour
2 tablespoons sugar
1 tablespoon melted butter
1/2 cup milk

In a large bowl, combine oatmeal, 3/4 cup of the rye flour, sugar and butter.

Slowly add the milk until a sticky dough forms. Add remaining rye flour and knead until the dough stiffens.

Wrap in saran wrap and chill for 1 hour.

Roll out dough to 1/4 inch thickness.

Cut into shapes.

Place cookie shapes on lightly greased cookie sheets.

Bake in oven at 350 degrees for about 15 minutes.
Turn off oven and let cookies cool in the oven.

Tip: Don't overindulge your dog with any treats. Small tidbits will keep his appetite good for his regular meals.

This recipe was taken from the book called "Make Your Own Dog Treats" The book offers 35 dog treat recipes, plus over 75 dog breed template cut-outs to use as cookie cutters. Ask for the book at your favorite bookseller. The ISBN is 978-1477518755 It has 130 pages.

Treat Canister

This is a fun project for you to make me a canister to put my treats in.

Here are the items you'll need:

An empty potato chip or nut canister with the lid.
Glue
Pictures of Dogs
Scissors

Look for pictures of dogs in some old magazines or newspapers. You can even use wrapping paper. Or you can draw some pictures of dogs yourself.

Be careful using the scissors and cut out the dogs. Leave a small edge of the paper around the dogs.

Put glue on the backsides of the dog pictures and place the pictures on the canister in a hodge podge mixed-up way with the corners and edges of the paper overlapping.

When the canister is completely covered with dogs, then apply a thin layer of glue over the top of the pictures and let dry before using.

Fill with my favorite treats.

Write your dog's name on the line on the food and water bowls.

Can you draw some food in the food bowl?

Be sure to wash your dog's bowls often to keep them clean.

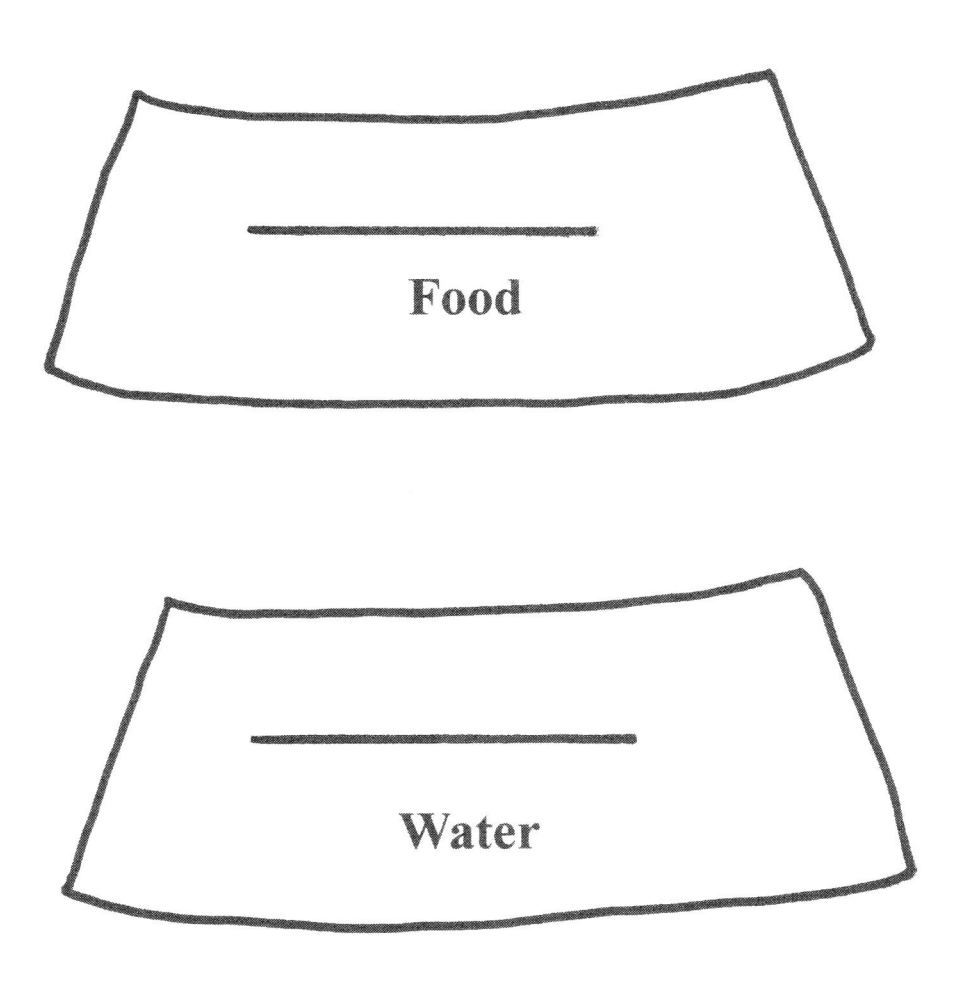

_____
Food

_____
Water

Teething and Chewing

Dogs and puppies have teeth and we use them for chewing and eating our food.

Puppies go through a stage of what is called teething, this is when their permanent teeth come in at about 16 to 30 weeks of age. At this time, you'll want to give me some extra tough toys that I can chew on.

The best toys will be either hard rubber toys or hard bones made of nylon. Don't give me real meat bones. These can splinter and cause me all kinds of intestinal problems.

I can also chew on some large knotted ropes. You can buy these at the pet store.

Puppies should never be allowed to bite and chew on your hands or feet. This may seem cute when I am little, but it is a bad habit that can lead to all sorts of problems for me. Do right by me, and teach me that this is not good dog behavior. Tell me "no" in a stern low voice if I start to bite at you or anyone else.

Playing tug of war is also not recommended. It looks like fun but it can cause me to become a little aggressive, even though I look like I am only playing.

Don't let anyone pull my tail or my ears, even in a playful manner. This can scare me and cause me to growl, nip or even bite.

A dog's teeth can administer quite the bite and be very painful.

No matter how big or how little I am, teach me that biting is not allowed.

You may have to consult with a dog trainer if you are not able to teach me not to bite.

Spay and Neuter

To have your dog spay or neutered will require a surgery that your veterinarian will perform.

This surgery will prevent your dog from having any puppies.

Before surgery your veterinarian will advise you not to feed or give me any water a few hours before surgery. Follow their advice so that I don't become ill during or after the surgery.

When you take me home from the veterinarian's office, you'll also be instructed on how much activity I should have. I will need to take it easy for a few days to recover from the surgery. I won't be running and jumping with you. I will need my rest, but I may still want you close to me. Now is a good time to read a book or story to me.

I will need a follow-up appointment with the veterinarian to be sure that I am healing from the surgery.

In no time, I'll be back to my old self and ready to play.

Grooming

You can take pride in grooming me and keeping me looking and smelling my best.

I like being clean. You can help me in so many ways to be sure that all my grooming needs are being met.

Start off with combing or brushing me often. I'll learn to like the attention and it will help us bond and I'll look forward to these sessions.

You can take me to a professional dog groomer on a regular basis, but between these grooming sessions, you can keep me looking good with minimum of care.

Use one special spot for my grooming. Having all of your grooming tools in this area will keep you from having to run and get something that you forgot. You can either set me on a table or on your lap.

Start slowly and talk to me. Use a comb or brush and be gentle. You may need to steady me with one hand, until I get used to this.

Putting down some treats for me to eat will keep me occupied while you brush me.

I have tender skin and any pain will cause me to not like the grooming that I should have. So don't comb me too hard.

Check my feet often for any sores or broken toenails.

I really like to be clean. So giving me a bath when I'm dirty or smelly will get me back to being clean. I may not like my baths at first. This can be scary for me. So go slow. Talk to me gently. Fill the sink or bathtub with a few inches of warm water. Or you can buy a plastic basin to be used just for my baths. Put down a towel or washcloth in the water for me to stand on and get some traction under my feet. This will make me feel more secure and not be too afraid.

Wet my body slowly with water from a cup. Don't pour the water over my head. Getting your hands wet and rubbing them over my head is much better and you won't get water or shampoo in my eyes or nose. Try not to splash.

Once I am wet, apply the puppy shampoo to my body and legs. Rinse well to remove all the shampoo from my body. If you are applying a cream rinse to me, now is the time for that. Then rinse me again.

Lift me out of the sink or bathtub and wrap me in a towel. Then watch the fun begin. I love this part of my bathing routine. I'll burrow into the towel and dry myself off by rolling around. Keep me out of drafts so I don't catch a cold.

If given time to get used to my baths, I can really come to enjoy them. These baths will bring lots of laughter from you and fun for the both of us.

For quick cleanings, check at the pet store for some special wipes that you can rub over me. This is a quick way to clean me when I'm not too dirty or you are short on time.

The other routine grooming care I will need is to be sure my toenails are cut if I haven't worn them down. If I am allowed to dig, I'll naturally wear down my front toenails. But my back feet will need your help. Also, if I have a dew claw on my front feet, that claw will need to be cut. You will not want to cut too much off, as you may cut into the quick and make my toenail bleed. If I have clear nails, you'll be able to see the pink quick on close inspection. Black nails are hard to see the quick, so get some expert help until you feel that you can handle this. The pet store does have some medicine that you can put on my toenails to stop the bleeding, just in case you cut too close.

The pet store will have special toenail clippers that are made just for dogs.

Take your time on our grooming sessions. Check my ears for possible mites. Don't be digging in my ears with cotton swabs or objects. If you notice a crusty substance or a foul odor in my ears, having me checked out by your favorite veterinarian will prove helpful. While checking my ears, you may not actually see any mites, as they are pretty small. So check for any crusty and foul odors. Your veterinarian has a trained eye and the proper equipment to help relieve me of any mites, should I get any. If mites are found in my ears or on my body, you'll need to treat me, my bed, and any areas that I have been allowed to roam in. You'll want to kill off any mite eggs so I don't get mites again once they hatch. Talk to the veterinarian and follow the advice they give you.

Also check me over for fleas and ticks. You'll be able to buy a special flea comb that will trap the fleas in the comb. This is a slower way to get rid of the fleas, but I'll enjoy the extra attention.

While checking me over, give my eyes a good look. If they are watery or have a discharge or crust, have your veterinarian take a look at me for a proper diagnosis.

You can make my own grooming kit with the following items. Keep them all together and only use them on me.

Comb
Brush
Flea comb
Old socks, rags or cotton balls
Basin for baths
Cup for baths
Dog shampoo
Dog creme rinse
Bath wipes
Toe nail clippers - made especially for dogs
Medicine to stop bleeding toenails
Old towels and paper towels
Special treats used only for when you are grooming me.
Any other medicines that your veterinarian has prescribed for me.

Wash my grooming supplies when they become dirty.

Throw out any rags or wipes that you used for mites, fleas, ticks or sores.

Bugs

In the grooming section I talked just briefly about fleas and ticks.

These bugs cause an untold amount of torment for dogs. If I have them you will no doubt know it. I'll be biting and scratching at myself the whole day and night. They can make sleeping almost non-existent for me.

These bugs will bite at my body and suck my blood.

Lice are another annoying bug that will bite and suck my blood.

Mites are very tiny bugs which will cause my skin to get irritated and my hair can fall out. You may not see the mites, as they can be under my skin.

If you notice any bugs on me, get a proper diagnosis as to what type of bug it is. Then you'll be able to treat me and kill the bugs. You will also need to clean everywhere that I have been to get rid of any of the eggs that the bugs have laid. If you don't vacuum up the eggs and destroy them, they will hatch and I'll be covered in bugs once again. This is time consuming but it must be done.

Ticks are a bug that you will be able to see. They will normally be stuck to me with their heads burrowed down into my skin. You will need to remove these ticks from my body. Use gloves and a tweezers. Don't use your bare hands.

Always check me over for ticks after we have come back from a romp in the woods, forest or the ocean. If ticks are especially bad in your area, ask your veterinarian about a pesticide that you could put on me before we go into the woods, this will help repel the ticks to keep them off of me.

Check with the pet store or the veterinarian for a complete system of bug killers. You will need shampoos, sprays and powders to rid me and your house of these pests.

Color Me

Toys

You know how much fun toys are for you and they'll be fun for me as well.

I should have my own toys to play with and chew on. If I don't have my own toys, then I will just pick up something that I find and chew on that.

When I have my own toys it is much easier to teach me not to pick up any other objects that are not mine.

If I should happen to pick up one of your shoes, tell me "no" and offer me one of my own toys. Praise me when I take my toy.

Toss my toys for me to chase. Encourage me to bring it back to you. Tell me to "drop it" and gently take the toy from me and toss it again. Before too long I will drop the toy on my own in the hopes that you toss it again for me to chase.

Toys can mean different things to me. If you give me a special toy when it is time to go in my crate or pen, I'll soon learn that this toy is my napping buddy.

Other toys can mean we are going outside for a good work out. Some toys are made for fetching and some toys are made for just laying down and chewing on them in a nice quiet place. These chewing toys work well when you are wanting to sit and read a book.

Giving me a toy box for all my toys and switching them around so I don't get bored with them is a nice way to keep my toys put away and to keep things tidy.

As I look into my toy box it won't take long for me to pick out my favorite ones to play with.

We'll spend a lot of hours playing together which will build a strong bond between us and will give me the exercise that I need.

Collar and Leash

Every well trained puppy will need a collar and a leash.

By the time I am grown up, I may have outgrown a few collars and may need a stronger leash.

Breaking me to a collar is pretty easy. Take me to the pet store and have them fit me with a proper size collar. You don't want one that is too big or I might get a foot caught in it. If you get one that is too small, I may have trouble breathing with it on.

There are many types of collars and even harnesses. If you are not sure which one to get me, ask at the pet store for their recommendation.

You'll also notice some collars come in either a chain variety, leather or even heavy cloth like material. Any type of collar that tightens when pulled, should never be left on me without constant supervision. Many of these types of collars are only meant for training exercises, not for everyday wear.

Once you purchase my harness or collar and leash, then take me home and put my collar or harness on me.

I may whine a little and try to scratch the collar off with my back foot. Give me one of my special toys to play with and within a short period of time I'll forget all about the collar or harness.

When I'm feeling good about the collar or harness and I am no longer trying to get it off, attach my leash to my collar or harness. Don't pull on the leash, just let me drag it around. Keep me occupied with a toy so that I don't try to chew on the leash. Do this everyday for a couple of days, then you can pick up the leash end and gently tug the leash and call me over to you.

Some puppies catch on to this without any trouble, others will balk once they feel the tug of the leash. Be patient with me and before long, I'll have forgotten what all the fuss was about and walk with you as proud as can be.

Chain Collar

Chain collars should only be used on your dog during training. These types of collars can tighten if they get caught on something and could strangle your dog. Use a flat leather or cloth buckle collar to put your dog's I.D. Tag on.

Here is how to assemble and put the chain collar on your dog.

Take one ring of the chain collar by holding it between the thumb and the index finger of one hand. Take the other ring with the other hand and pull the chain upward to its longest size. Then lower the chain to fall into the inside of the lower ring, this will form the loop.

When you put the chain collar over your dog's head, the ring that is free and has the chain sliding through the other ring should be on the right side of your dog's neck. If you have put the collar on properly you'll be able to test it to be sure that it loosens the moment that you let go of it. Pull on the ring and then let go to see if it loosens. If it stays tight you have put the collar on wrong. Take it off and try it again.

You might also practice making the chain loop and slipping it over your wrist. You'll be able to test it to see if it releases immediately when you let go of it.

That's all there is to it. Now we are ready to train.

Training Chart

Below is a chart for you to keep track of the training progress that your dog is learning.

Only teach me one command at a time. When I learn that command, practice it often, then start to teach me another command.

Keep my training lessons short, lasting about 10 minutes each, and do the lessons 2 or 3 times each day, and always end on a happy note and tell me how smart I am. Praise me and give me a nice treat.

Each command could take me about a week to fully understand what you are trying to teach me. Be patient and make my training sessions fun. Before long, you'll be so proud of me and you can be proud of yourself too, for training me to be so smart and well mannered.

Put a tiny check mark in each practice box. There are 3 boxes to practice 3 times per day. When I have been taught the command and you can see that I am responding to your command, write the date in the "I Know It" box.

Command	Practice	Practice	Practice	I Know It
Come				
Sit				
Stay				
Lie Down				
Heel				
Stand				

Collars

Below are two collars. Your pet supply store will help you to fit me with the proper size.

The chain collar should only be used for training purposes, do not leave it on me when I am not being supervised or trained.

The flat collar can be used for my everyday wear that you'll attach my I.D. Tag to.

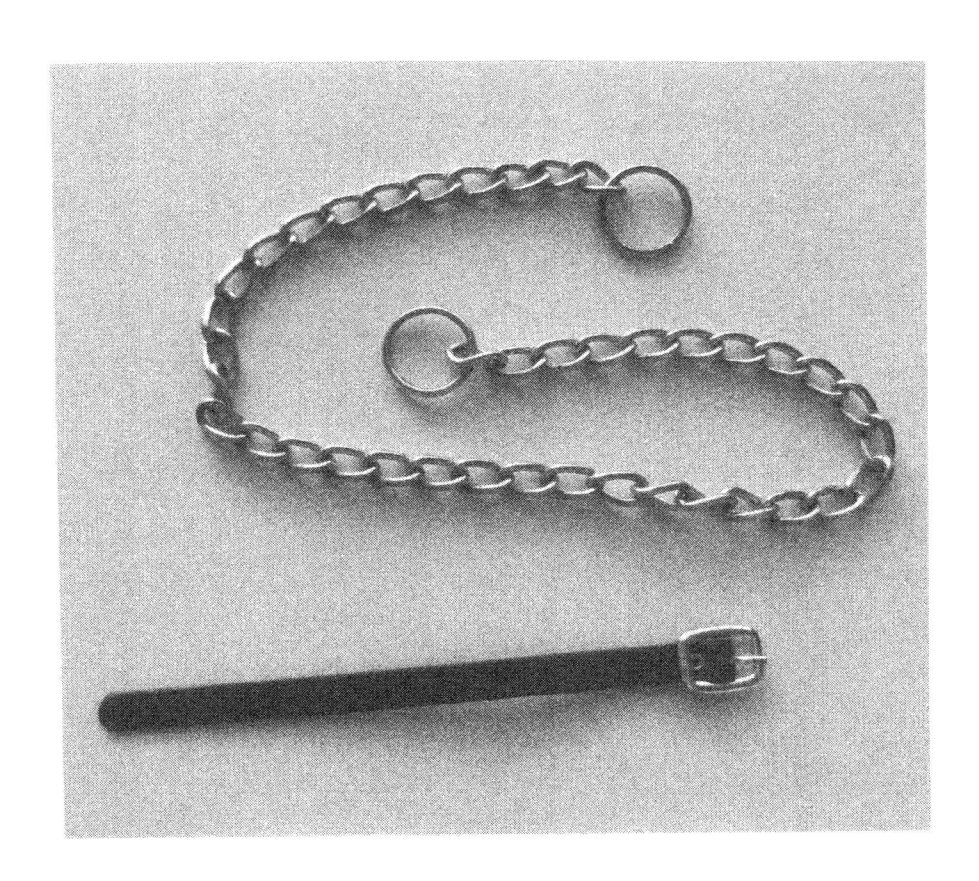

Below is a chain collar that is ready to be used. When facing your dog the collar will slip over it's head and the long loose end will come from the top side of your dog's neck and the end that the leash will attach to will be on your dog's right side.

Obedience Training

Every good dog should know the 5 basic obedience commands. They are Come, Sit, Stay, Lie Down and Heel.

If your puppy is young, some of the formal training will not take place until it is older.

The one command to teach and work on everyday is the word "come."

This could potentially save your dog's life one day. He must learn to obey this command, each and every time you say it.

Never call your puppy or dog over to you to punish it. NEVER!

Every time your puppy obeys your command to "come" should be a happy time. Praise your puppy and offer a treat.

Practice this everyday, even while I am small or young. Attach a long light weight cord to my collar, then let me wander away from you. When you tell me to "come," start to reel me in with the cord. Praise me when I get to you.

The formal obedience training can start after I am about 4 months old and I have gotten all of my puppy shots. Then you can take me to a training class where other pups and dogs will be present along with their owners. The trainer will be able to show you how to hold my leash, where I should walk, and how to teach me to sit, stay and lie down.

Dog trainers should train with the point of view of "positive reinforcement" rather than from a "punish and conquer" attitude.

Ask around for a recommendation from other dog owners to see if they know a good dog trainer in your area.

A well trained dog is a pleasure to own and I really want to make you proud of me.

Teaching The Come Command

Long before I start any formal obedience training you can start to teach me the "come" command.

This is probably the most useful command to teach me. It is a pretty easy command to teach me just by practicing everyday at home. The "come" command could potentially save my life, but I must respond to it each and every time that you request me to "come". Responding to the "come" command will be easy for me to do in everyday situations, but when I am seeing something that seems more interesting, I may not listen to you. So practice this often at home and in other crowded situations, such as a dog park.

First off, you must never call me over to you and then tell me how bad I am. Don't yell at me or hit me. This will only make me not want to come to you.

Always be cheerful when you are calling me to "come".

Treats and praise will go along way in helping me to learn this command.

Start off by attaching a long cord to my collar. Hold one end of the cord and let me wander away from you. You can use my name and the word "come" when you are ready to train me. Don't confuse me by adding different words. Don't use "come here" or "get over here". Don't call me in a gruff mad voice either.

Once I have wandered away from you, in a very cheerful voice tell me to "come". At the same time start to reel me in with the long cord. Once I reach you, praise me and give me a treat. Tell me how good I am.

You can practice this outside and inside the house.

As I get better and come to you each time that you give me the "come" command, start to work with me at times that are more distracting to me. Such as when I am chewing on a dental bone or one of my favorite toys.

Having someone else entering your house can be distracting to me too. So ask a friend to help you out and come over to distract me. Be sure that I have on the long cord. Let your friend come in the house and immediately you are to tell me to "come". Have your friend ignore me. Reel me in if needed and praise me and offer me a treat.

As I get better you can have your friend sit down and pet me. Then call me again to you, using the "come" command.

You can practice this with different people and even if your friend has a dog that they could bring over with them.

Once you can see that I am obeying your command to "come" you can take off the long cord. If I should ignore you when you call me to "come" then put the cord back on me and practice with me some more.

Practice the "come" command everyday. Call me when I am in another room and away from you. Give me lots of praise and a treat.

Call me when I am just lying across the room from you. Again, give me lots of praise and a treat. I will learn that coming to you is a good thing and that I should respond each and every time to your calling.

Use the chart in your book to monitor my practice lessons and before long you'll be proud of how smart I am when I learn the "come" command.

Teaching The Heel Command

Put my collar and leash on me. Be sure to have some tasty treats for me so you can reward me when I have done a good job.

Dogs should walk on your left side. They should not be behind you or ahead of you. They should not be pulling on the leash when you are trying to walk, or trying to jump on people that are walking by or at other dogs.

Start with me on your left side. Put your left foot forward first and take off at a brisk walk. Tell me to "heel" at the same time that you start to walk. Keep my leash fairly short, so I don't run ahead or lag behind. If you need you can give me a slight tug to hurry me up, or to slow me down. Repeat the "heel" command a few times during our walk and especially every time that you need to give me a tug to get me into the correct heeling position.

My head should be about even with your knee. If I try to get ahead, be patient and keep me on your left side and give me a slight tug.

We can practice this everyday. As I get better at walking on your left side, you can give me a little more leash and you will not have to keep it so short in order to keep me in the correct position. If I start to wander ahead of you, or lag behind you, tug me slightly and repeat the command "heel".

When we are walking forward, go about 10 steps and turn to your right and go in the other direction, give me a tug to keep up with you, and tell me to "heel". When I am in the correct position, a little tasty treat would be nice and don't forget to tell me what a good dog I am.

Once I have mastered the right turn, you'll need to work on the left turn. This can be a littler trickier as now you will need to sort of step in front of me in order to get me to turn. I may bump into your leg at first. This will cause me to keep an eye on you so that I can be prepared for your turns.

Each time you turn, give me the "heel" command.

Before long you'll be able to work on a complete about face and turn and go in the complete opposite direction.

As I get better at the "heel" command, you can walk at different speeds. Walk fast, then slow, and you can even stop for a few minutes.

At every speed, you will want me to be on your left side. Even if we are running. Don't let me slip back into trying to run ahead of you. Having me run ahead of you is actually dangerous. If I should suddenly stop, you will trip and fall right over me and both of us could get hurt.

Keep these lessons short. Three times a day for about 10 minutes each time should be plenty.

Keep my lessons fun. Praise me when I have done a good job.

Don't get discouraged if I don't seem to be catching on to what you want me to do. I really do want to please you, and learning will just take time.

If you practice with me everyday, I will learn. But don't practice one day and then take a week off. This will make it harder for me to remember what you are trying to teach me.

Before long you'll see an improvement in how well I am doing.

End every lesson on a happy note. Praise me and give me a treat.

Teaching The Sit Command

Whenever you start to teach me a new command, start our training lesson by practicing some of the commands that I have already learned.

Teaching me the "sit" command can be started right after I learn the "heel" command.

While we are walking and practicing the "heel" command, you'll want to have my leash in your right hand. This will keep your left hand free.

When we come to a stop, simply pull up on my leash with your right hand, and with your left hand push down gently on my rump, and tell me to "sit".

This should be done in one easy movement. Practice this everyday, three times a day for about 10 minutes. Just walk, stop and pull up on my leash and push down on my rump, all the while telling me to "sit". It is that easy.

You can also reinforce the "sit" command, when I am not on the leash and we are not walking. Having one of my tasty treats in your hand, hold the treat just over my head, so that I can see it, and move your hand slightly so that I have to tip my head back in order to keep my eyes on the treat. Tell me to "sit" and give me the treat when I do.

Only do these "sit" reinforcements once I have learned the "sit" command while I am on my leash, otherwise I will try to jump up and get the treat without knowing what you are trying to teach me.

You can practice this with you standing in front of me or with me on your left side.

"Sit" is an easy command to teach me. I'll catch on really quick if you will practice with me everyday.

Praise me when I have done a good job and reward me with a treat.

Teaching The Stay Command

The "stay" command is one of the easiest commands to teach me.

Put my collar and leash on me. Stuff my training treats in your pocket.

Have me on your left side. Practice the commands that I have already learned, such as "come", "heel" and "sit". Praise me and have my treats ready for when I do a good job. Work on the commands that I already know for about 5 minutes before starting to train me on the "stay" command.

With me sitting on your left side, have the leash in your left hand, use your right foot to take a step in front of me and at the same time using your left hand pull slightly back on my leash to keep me from moving forward and with your right hand swing it right in front of my face in an open fashion and tell me to "stay". Quickly step in front of me and turn and face me. If I move, tell me again to "stay" and put me back in my sitting position.

Stand up and practice this move all by yourself, without me. The movements should all come quick and easy. When you can visualize the movements and feel that you can do them easily, then you can proceed to train me.

Practice the "stay" command a few times. Reward me with a special treat when I have done well.

Once you can see that I am catching on to this you can attempt to step further away from me. While you are standing directly in front of me, put your hand up and out from your body, and tell me to "stay" and take a step backwards. Keep your hand up, to remind me of the "stay" command. Only stand away from me for a few seconds, and then come back to me. Praise me if I did not get up.

Practice this until you can get to the end of my leash, while I "stay". Start to make the time a little longer each time that you give me the "stay" command, before you come back to me.

Work on the "stay" command everyday for about a week. By then I should know how to "stay" pretty well. You should be able to walk away from me and then back to me.

Now you can practice the "stay" command along with the "come" command. Have me "sit" and "stay". Walk backwards to the end of my leash, have me wait for a few seconds and then command me to "come". Give me a slight tug on my leash if you need to get me moving towards you. Once I come to you, have me "sit" in front of you by giving me the "sit" command. You may need to tug slightly up and back on my leash to get me to "sit".

Once I have learned these commands well, you can mix my training up some so that I don't anticipate what you are going to say next.

Make me "come" and "sit" in front of you. Then tell me to "stay" and walk away from me.

Practice the "stay" command at other times during the day. You can use the "stay" command when someone comes to the front door and you open the door to let them in or to talk to them. The "stay" command will keep me from running out the front door. You may need to keep my collar and leash on me while we are at the door until I learn the "stay" command and will obey you.

As always, end my lesson on a good note and praise me and give me a special treat.

Use the chart in your book to write down the progress that we are making.

I'm sure you are getting excited to see that I am learning these commands.

I really am smart and I want to learn and know the rules.

Teaching The Lie Down Command

The wording you use for the "lie down" command is important so that you don't mix them up with other training words.

If your dog jumps up on you and you use the word "down" to teach me not to jump on you, then the word "down" will get me confused when you try to teach me to "lie down" on command.

A better word to use when I try to jump on you is the word "off".

Use either "down" or "lie down" to teach me the "lie down" command. Lay will sound to much like "stay".

Start my training session by putting on my collar and leash. Get those tasty treats of mine in your pocket so that you'll be ready to offer me one when I do well.

Begin by going through all the other commands that you have taught me. Praise me and offer me a tiny treat when I have done them well.

You may notice that the more you train me, the easier the training gets. This is because now I am getting a better idea that you are wanting me to do something. You may even notice that I am paying more attention to you too.

After you have gone through all the other commands that I have learned, start me on your left side. Tell me to "sit" and to "stay" and take a step forward and turn around to face me.

Now stoop down and gently put your left hand over my shoulders and push down and at the same time pull gently on my leash towards the ground. Tell me to "lie down". Sometimes a little treat right at my nose will help to bring me closer to the ground. When I am in the down position, tell me to "stay". Keep me in this position for a few seconds. Tell me how good I am. Praise me and offer me a treat.

Go back to my right side and I'll be in the heeling position. Practice the "heel" command. Stop and tell me to "sit" and repeat the procedure for the "lie down" command.

This is a good command to teach me. So practice this three times everyday for about 10 minutes each time.

Write down in our training chart each time that we practice this.

Once I learn the "lie down" command, you can easily have me lay at your feet while you read a book or do your homework.

Remember to end our training session on a happy note. Praise me well and offer me a treat.

Teaching The Stand Command

This is a useful command to teach me. It can be useful when you are trying to groom me and need me to stand so that you can tend to my grooming needs. It will also help when I am at the veterinarians office when they need to examine me.

It is also a very easy command to teach me.

Put on my collar and leash and grab some of my training treats and put them in your pocket.

Practice the other commands that I have already learned. Run me through these commands for about 10 minutes. Then put me in a "sit-stay". With you by my side, simply bend down and slip a hand under my belly and gently nudge me upward and tell me to "stand". Keep your hand under my belly to prevent me from sitting back down. Have me hold this position for about 10 seconds. Praise me and give me a treat.

Start walking again and command me to "heel". Stop and repeat the "sit-stay" command and do the procedure again to get me to "stand".

Once I am catching on to this, you'll want to command me to "lie down" and teach me the "stand" command from the lying down position as well as the sitting position.

Don't forget to praise me and offer me a treat when I have done well.

Questions and Answers on Training

Here are a few questions on training your dog. I hope you get them all correct. You can read the previous chapters to learn the answers.

What is the command called when I walk on your left side? _____

Can you use treats to train me? _____

What could the "stand" command be used for? _____

Does yelling at me work to train me? _____

Should we practice our training everyday? _____

What is the command that could save my life? _____

Besides treats, what else helps in my training? _____

Missing Vowels

Below are some words that have missing vowels. Can you fill in the missing vowels for these words that pertain to training your dog?

Use these vowels   A – E – I – O – U – Y

TR _ _ N

TR _ _ T

S _ T

H _ _ L

C _ M _

L _ _ D _ WN

S T _ N D

L _ _ S H

C _ L L _ R

S T _ _

P R _ _ S _

S M _ R T

Unscramble These Training Words

Below are common words that are used in dog training.

Can you unscramble the letters to make real words?

RPAIES

EEHL

IST

TRNAI

TTERA

YSTA

OMCE

STDAN

LEAHS

OLLARC

PRACICTE

LEI DNOW

PAITENEC

LEONSS

TECHA

Word Find Puzzle on Training

Below is a word find puzzle that contains the words that you'll use to help train your dog. Circle the words and check them off the list when you find them.

PRAISE

TREAT

SIT

STAY

HEEL

COME

LIE DOWN

STAND

COLLAR

LEASH

B	P	R	A	I	S	E	R	W	A	T	R	B	U	J	S	I	T	T
A	Z	X	C	M	N	T	T	R	E	A	T	W	M	O	P	Y	O	O
R	D	S	T	A	Y	K	G	A	L	L	P	Q	F	S	H	E	E	O
F	B	V	D	O	G	A	Q	U	Y	Y	B	R	J	U	M	Y	D	D
Z	H	E	E	L	Z	L	H	U	Y	F	A	L	C	O	M	E	L	C
X	O	X	U	E	E	S	T	A	N	D	H	O	M	R	E	E	W	T
H	A	L	Y	E	Q	R	E	N	T	I	N	N	L	E	A	S	H	A
J	W	L	I	E	D	O	W	N	E	B	V	C	Q	Q	A	H	A	T
G	E	A	K	H	J	I	O	U	Y	W	C	O	L	L	A	R	K	L
Z	X	C	V	B	E	R	T	Y	O	O	P	V	T	R	A	N	N	I

Barking

Dogs bark! That is what we do. However, it can be troublesome to your family and to your neighbors if my barking is excessive and keeps them from sleeping or enjoying their home life.

Excessive barking is the number one reason that complaints are filed with the police or the dog pound.

Dogs will bark for a number of different reasons. Knowing what I am barking about will help you to train me.

If I am sitting and just barking or howling with my head up towards the sky I may just be bored or lonely. You should tell me "no" or "be quiet." You should take charge and be sure that my days are not boring. Maybe I need more playtime and exercise.

I will bark at strange people or other animals if they cross in front of my house or yard. This is me protecting my home. However, if after they are gone and I am still barking, this is taking the barking to the extreme. This will annoy your neighbors. So teach me that a few barks are fine, but not to carry on.

Dogs will also learn that when the doorbell rings or there is a knock on the front door, that those sounds are announcing a visitor. My barking will also announce the visitor. You will need to teach me not to run out the front door when you open it to let your visitor in. Attaching my leash to me and having me sit while you open the door will keep me safe.

Teach me what you want me to do when you allow the visitor into your home. Don't let me jump on them or become a pest. Don't let me bark at them uncontrolled. This is annoying for everyone.

Decide if I should lay down on a rug. Maybe you want me to go to my bed or crate while the visitor is with you. Or maybe your visitor has come over to play with both of us. Either way, don't let my barking become a nuisance.

Traveling

When traveling with me in the car, don't let me jump from seat to seat, or from window to window. This is unsafe.

Teach me to stay in one spot. You can buy a special dog seat belt for me to keep me in one spot, plus the seat belts can be used to keep me safe in case of an accident or a sudden stop.

I can also be transported in a dog crate. Put my favorite blanket in there along with my favorite toy.

Stop often for potty breaks and for me to stretch my legs.

Before going on vacation, assemble everything that I will need for the trip and put them all in one suitcase for me. Don't forget my food, my collar and leash, toys, blankets, my grooming supplies and especially any medicines if I have to take any. Make sure that my identification tag is up to date, and take along some temporary tags to update along the way on our trip.

You might also want to take along my health records that show when I last had my shots. Some places will require that I also have had a rabies shot.

Getting me accustomed to riding in the car long before a vacation trip is planned is a smart idea. Some dogs may not travel well and could vomit from being over anxious in the car. Your veterinarian can give me some medicine to soothe my tummy and help me relax.

Traveling with me can be fun, it just takes a little preparation to be sure everyone is safe and having a good time.

Color Me

Counting Paws

Can you count the puppy paws below and write the answers on each line?

🐾 + 🐾 🐾 = _____

🐾 🐾 + 🐾 🐾 = _____

🐾 🐾 + 🐾 🐾 🐾 = _____

🐾 🐾 🐾 + 🐾 🐾 = _____

🐾 🐾 + 🐾 🐾 🐾 = _____

How many puppy paws are on this whole page? _____

Health Issues

All dogs and puppies can have some health issues.

You can take me to the veterinarian to get my necessary shots. This will help prevent me from getting sick. Hopefully, I already have been started on the shots from the person you got me from.

We are also prone to parasites, both inside and outside of our body. These include, fleas, ticks, mites, lice and worms of all kinds.

Your best defense for me is to be sure that I have had my regular shots and worming. Keeping me on a regular schedule to see the veterinarian can protect me from many of these health issues that can effect all puppies and dogs.

Follow the advice from your veterinarian for preventive treatments and also for any remedies that can help me with any parasites that I get.

It is important that you don't let my toenails get overgrown.

Dogs and puppies are also prone to digestive disorders, such as, gas, bloat, diarrhea, constipation, and eating poisonous plants.

Some dogs will also eat sand and dirt, which will cause stomach problems.

Never feed me moldy or spoiled food.

Many digestive problems can be life threatening. Consult your veterinarian at once for a proper diagnosis and treatment.

Our teeth can also cause us problems. From having an abscess to needing my teeth scraped of any tartar.

Having too much tartar on my teeth will cause my breath to smell and it could also cause my teeth to fall out. You can have the veterinarian scrape my teeth, if chewing on dental treats doesn't help.

Puppies and dogs can also get diabetes and many types of allergies. If your dog starts any wheezing, have the veterinarian check it over for possible causes.

Diabetes in a dog or puppy can be treated, but it will take a special diet that your veterinarian can advise you on. It may even require daily shots of insulin.

Being overweight is also something that will cause me problems. Be sure I get daily exercise, even in bad weather.

Overfeeding me too many special treats may seem like a kindness, but it really isn't. I know that I have the most adorable face when I want an extra treat, but you must be strong and not give in when I am begging for more.

Having me checked for worms or other internal parasites will help rid me of these pesky creatures. Watch for ticks on my body too.

If I have a strong odor coming from my ears, have the veterinarian check me over for an infection.

With so many health problems you may wonder if I'll be healthy and happy all of my life. This will vary from dog to dog.

Do your best to give me the very best veterinarian care when I need it, but also yearly check-ups even when I'm feeling great is a good idea. Your veterinarian has a trained eye and can spot things that you won't be able to see. Catching any ailments early on, is better than waiting until they get real bad and out of control.

Water Hazards

There are a number of things that a new puppy can get into trouble with.

Bodies of water are one of them.

Yes, most puppies can swim. But some are not good swimmers and all of them should have close supervision around water. All dogs and puppies can get too tired or cold while swimming.

Swimming pools can be fun. Your puppy or dog will need to learn how to get out of the swimming pool if you have one. You can buy a special ramp so that your puppy can get a good grip with his feet to help him get out. To use this ramp your puppy or dog must be taught where it is and what it is used for. Show your puppy the ramp and practice as often as you can so that your puppy will know how to get out of the pool. These ramps can also be used with a boat.

Natural bodies of water such as oceans, lakes, ponds, creeks and rivers can have a strong undercurrent and can pull your puppy or dog too far out and you may never see me again.

If I am not a good swimmer, you can get me a life jacket at the pet store which will help me stay afloat while in the water.

Don't let me get too cold while I am swimming or fetching things in the water. Even if I am cold, sometimes the fun that I am having will just keep me from staying out of the water. You need to be in charge of my safety. If I am shivering, stop the water games and dry me off.

Watch for other hazards along the shore line too. Puppies and dogs are very curious as to what all those smells are and may try to pick objects up that they find. Fish hooks can cause me a lot of pain. I may get one of these in my mouth or stuck on one of my paws. We also have a bad habit of rolling in stinky dead fish that have come ashore. Teach me the word "yuck" to stay away from them. Water games are fun, but they should come with rules.

Missing Vowels

Here are more puzzles that you can do. Fill in the missing vowels from the words below. Some of the words pertain to what dogs and puppies like to eat and do, and the last two words are what your dog should have plenty of when he is outside.

Use these vowels: A – E – I – O – U - Y

B _ R K

P _ P P _

T _ _ T H

P _ W S

F _ T C H

_ _ T

T _ N G _ _

_ _ R S

T R _ _ N

S L _ _ P

P L _ _

M _ _ T

S H _ D _

W _ T _ R

Word Find

Below is a word find puzzle. These words all pertain to puppies or dogs. Circle the words and check them off the list when you find them.

___ CLEAN

___ PUPPY

___ FUR

___ TEETH

___ PLAY

___ WATER

___ COLORS

___ FOOD

___ TRAIN

___ SLEEP

C	P	U	P	P	Y	N	E	O	N	A	G	O	N	N	N	M	T
H	A	F	R	E	Q	E	A	R	S	K	S	W	A	T	E	R	E
M	M	F	I	N	S	E	C	T	S	R	E	F	R	A	T	S	E
S	E	U	M	G	I	C	D	O	R	E	P	F	I	S	H	S	T
L	J	R	S	Y	T	L	F	D	V	B	S	A	R	G	U	O	H
E	I	H	W	Q	S	I	A	C	D	G	C	D	I	G	B	S	J
E	U	G	U	I	N	M	C	H	I	D	E	W	F	A	Z	X	X
P	M	T	M	V	K	B	J	Q	F	O	O	D	E	N	T	T	Y
T	R	A	I	N	S	U	L	A	N	W	C	L	E	A	N	D	E
P	L	A	Y	T	S	B	C	A	C	O	L	O	R	S	D	E	E

Is Your Dog a Blue Ribbon Winner?

Write your dog's name on the line in the ribbon, and color it blue.

1st Place

_____

Daily Care Chart

Below is a chart to help you remember to take care of me.

You may want to make some copies of the chart, before you start to use it. Then you'll have plenty for the year and you can hang it someplace where you'll see it to remind you about my daily care.

Put a little smiley face, star or check mark each time you have taken care of my needs. If I need to be fed twice a day, make two marks.

Playtime can include my daily walks, if you are allowed to do that. Otherwise, play with me in a safe place.

Change my water everyday.

Clean daily around my food dishes. This will keep ants and bugs away.

Shake out my bedding every week and give it a washing if it needs it.

Groom me every day.

	Sunday	Monday	Tuesday	Wednesday	Thursday	Friday	Saturday
Feed Me							
Water Me							
Playtime							
Groom Me							
Clean Daily							
Clean Weekly							

Identification

Just in case your dog or puppy ever gets lost, having a current means of identification is important.

You can buy a metal or plastic identification tag at the pet store, or through the mail from an animal supply catalog. Attach this tag to your dog's collar that it wears everyday.

Dogs can also be tattooed in their ear or inner leg.

Your veterinarian can also put a tiny microchip under your dog's skin. This microchip can only be read with a special machine. So that anyone who finds your dog would need to take your dog to a veterinarian or some animal control place in order to read the microchip.

There are technologies that will even scan an identification tag from many mobile phones.

A temporary tag can be made of paper and filled out with the important information on how to contact you, if someone finds your dog. These paper tags can be covered with clear tape and are perfect if you are traveling and need to update your motel room, lodging, camp ground, or a friend or relatives phone number.

Take a picture of your dog and keep it in a safe place just in case you need to print up some "lost dog" fliers. You can then pass these fliers out to other people to help you find your lost dog.

Hopefully I never get lost, but it is better to be prepared for my safe return.

Unscramble These Letters

These words all pertain to dogs. Can you unscramble the letters?

RFU

LCKI

PWAS

EXCISEER

EASHL

RCOLLA

RTECA

BTHA

RAITN

TTEEH

GMOORNIG

YPLA

VETNAIARERIN

CNAIEN

WTARE

SHEAD

Taking Me Outdoors

Taking me outdoors everyday for some exercise and fresh air is a lot of fun for me.

If you have a fenced yard you can let me off my leash and let me run and play.

Bring my favorite fetching toys for me to chase.

Keep an eye out for any dangers in the yard. Be aware of anything that could fall over on me.

Keep me away from plants. Some of these can be poisonous if I eat them.

If you live in an area where there are birds of prey such as, hawks, eagles, or owls, keep an eye out for them so they don't try to get me.

Other wild animals can also be a threat to me. Foxes, wolves, skunks, coyotes, badgers and even large snakes. If you see any of these animals while I am playing outside, take me back indoors until they leave the area.

If you don't have a fenced yard for me to run in, always be sure that I keep my collar and leash on. This will keep me safe from moving vehicles or to keep me from running off and getting lost.

While I am outside always be sure that I have access to fresh cool water and plenty of shade if it is hot outside. I can get overheated and could possibly die.

These outings are fun and I'll make you laugh at my cute antics while we play and enjoy the great outdoors. Let's do this often, okay?

Tails

Dogs have different types of tails. Some are short and some are long. Can you circle the tail below that most resembles your dog's tail?

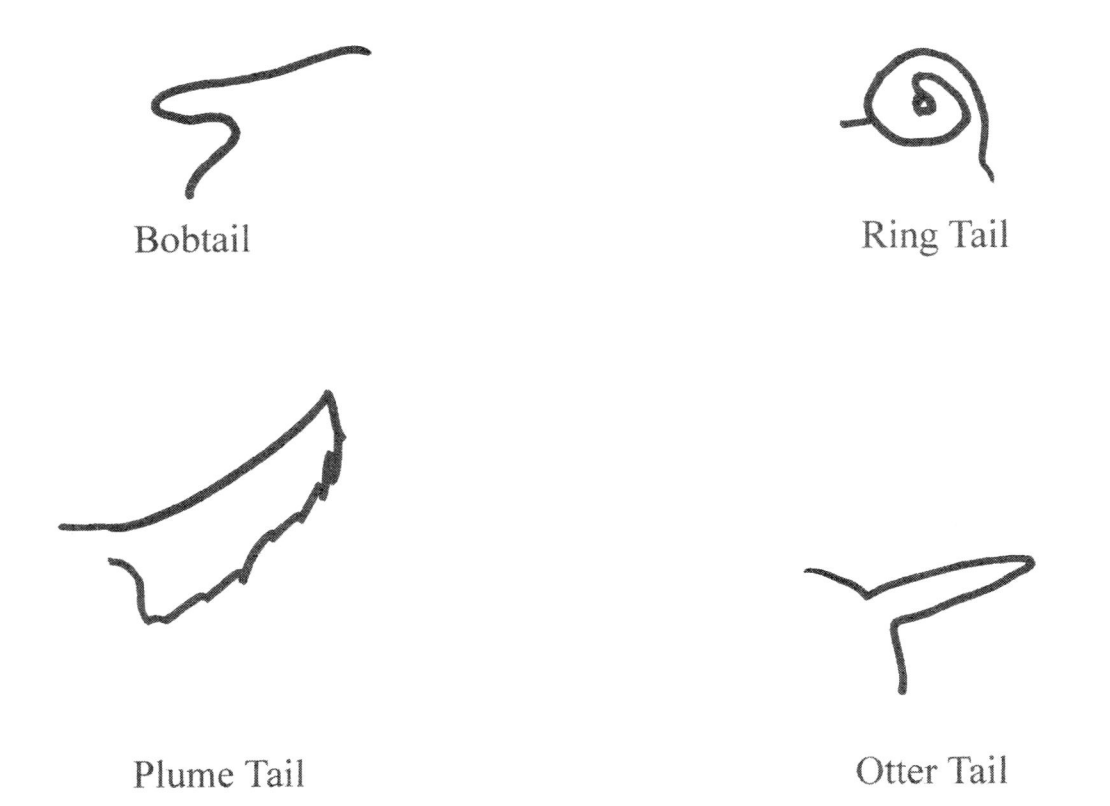

Bobtail

Ring Tail

Plume Tail

Otter Tail

Gay Tail

Screw Tail

More Tails

Whip Tail

Bushy Tail

Tail with a Pom Pom

Ears

Dogs have different types of ears. There are six different types below. Can you circle the ear that most resemble your dog's ears?

Prick Ear

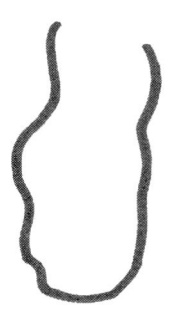

Drop Ear

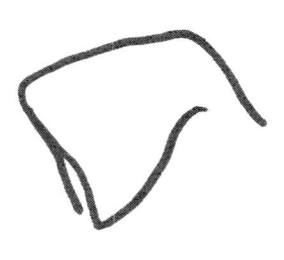

Button Ear

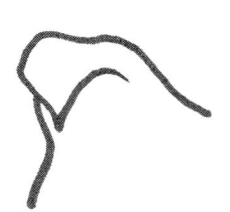

Semi-Prick Ear

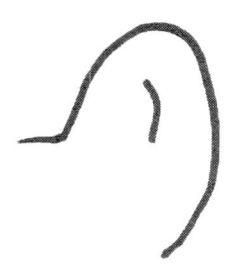

Bat Ear

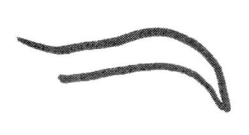

Rose Ear

Paw Print Paper Weight

Here is an easy recipe to make your own paw print paper weight using your dog's paw. You might want to paint your dog's name on the paper weight when it is all dry.

    2 cups of white flour

    1 / 2 cup of salt

    3 /4 cup of water

Mix the ingredients together and knead for about 15 minutes. The dough will be very stiff.

Flatten into a circle, about 1 /2 inch thick, and have your dog step in the center to leave his or her paw print.

Bake at 300 degrees for about 20 minutes or until nice and golden brown.

Let cool. The dough will harden as it cools.

When cool you can paint the paper weight and add your dog's name.

Make Your Own Note Cards

On the next page you will find two different pictures for you to make your own note cards.

Carefully tear the page out of your book. Cut on the dotted line and trim the edge that was torn out of your book.

Fold the paper in half.

Color the pictures and add any bones, balls, toys etc.

Add your own wording on the inside, such as, Happy Birthday, Get Well Soon or whatever else you'd like.

Give the note card to someone special.

Made For
You By: _____

Made For
You By: _____

Make Your Own Bookmarks

Below are three bookmarks. Cut out and write your dog's name on one end and color them in nice bright colors for your books. If you cover them with clear mailing tape, it will make them sturdy.

I Love

I Love

I Love

After you cut out your bookmarks, draw a picture of your dog on the backside of each bookmark. Then color them before covering them with clear tape.

Puppy Maze

Puppies like biscuits and food. Will you draw your puppy, a biscuit and a bowl of food? Then help your puppy find his way to the biscuit and the food through the maze.

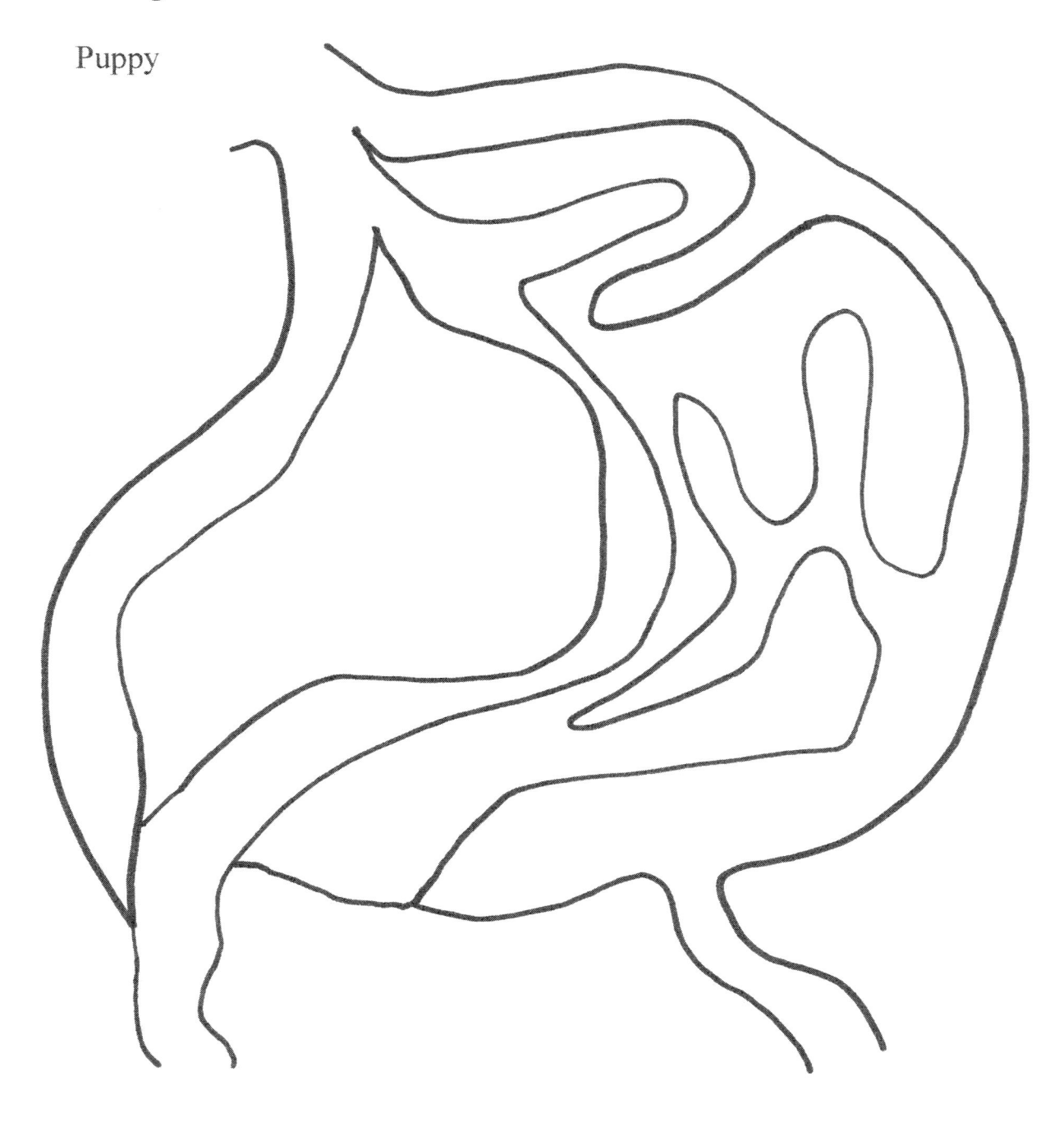

Puppy

Biscuit

Bowl of Food

Fun and Games

Even though we'll have a great time together with all of my obedience training, housebreaking, walks and grooming, we'll still have plenty of time for some fun and games.

Tricks are taught the same way that my obedience commands are. Practice the tricks daily. You'll need to repeat the word that you want to use for the trick that you want to teach me. Many tricks are taught as an extension from the obedience commands. So teaching me the commands first, will help in teaching me any tricks. Plus, I'll need plenty of praise and those tasty treats always get my attention.

Shake Hands. This will impress your friends and is fairly easy for me to learn. There are two ways to teach me to shake hands. Tell me to "sit". Kneel down in front of me and simply take my paw in your hand, and at the same time tell me to "shake hands". Give my paw a little shake. Give me a treat and praise me. Repeat a couple of times. The second way is to kneel down in front of me and with one hand touch me at the shoulder and push slightly to tip me off balance. As I lean over, one of my front paws will come up off the ground. At the same time that you give me the command "shake hands" you'll simply grab my paw that is off the ground. Praise me well and offer me a treat. Repeat this a couple of times too. It won't take long and you won't have to tip me off balance.

Roll Over. The treats will really help with this trick. While facing me, tell me to "lie down". Kneel down in front of me and with one hand, that you have a treat in, let me sniff it and with your other hand simply roll my body over and my nose and my head should follow your hand with the treat in. Tell me to "roll over". Praise me and offer me that tasty treat. It will help if you put the hand with the treat just off center of my body and slightly up so that I have to cock my head a little. This will help in rolling me over. Practice this a few times.

Jump Through a Hoop. You can teach me this by putting me in a room. Take a large hoop and hold it in between the doorway. Keep the hoop touching the floor at first. You can lure me through the hoop with a tasty treat, and tell me to "jump", just as I come through the hoop. You can also lure me through the hoop with the word "come". Then as I come through the hoop tell me to "jump". I'll catch on to this in no time. As I get better, raise the hoop a few inches off of the floor. Once I know this trick you can do it anywhere in the house, not just in front of the doorways.

Close The Door. This is not just a fun trick to know, but it can be very useful too. While we are in a room together, leave the door open just a few inches. Bring me in front of the door. With a treat in your hand, put your hand just up over my nose and real close to the door. Encourage me to get the treat. If I am not too big, you can help rest my front paws on the door, to help close it. Tell me in a happy voice, "close the door", just as the door moves shut. This will take a little practice. Reward me with the treat and praise me. Be sure that while I am learning this, that my paws don't get caught in the door when it is shutting.

Begging This trick is really cute when I am sitting more on my haunches and sitting up with my front paws in the air. To start, just tell me to "sit". Then with a treat in one hand, put your hand up over my head and with your other hand, help my front feet get off the ground. At the same time, tell me to "beg". Praise me and offer me the treat. If I should get up and stand, just repeat the "sit" command and keep practicing with me.

Fetch	Most dogs love to play fetch. Sometimes we may not bring the ball or item back until we realize that you will throw it again, which makes the whole game more fun. You can teach me this really easy just by tossing a favorite toy away from me and saying "fetch". Encourage me to bring it back. You may need to use the "come" command so that I return to you. Then you will need to teach me to "give" or "drop it". When I return to you, tell me to "sit-stay". Then gently take the toy or ball in your hand and tell me to "give", as you take the ball or toy from me. Throw the toy again, and tell me to "fetch". Most of the time, treats are not needed for this game, but a nice praising of "good dog" is in order.
Go Find	This is fun and keeps my mind active. Start by just letting me see you hide a toy or treat. Tell me to "go find" and encourage me to seek out the toy or treat. As I get better at this, you can tell me what to find. Such as "go find your ball" or "go find your squeaky toy". You'll be surprised at how I can tell the toys apart. Especially with lots of practice. You can put me into a "sit-stay" command before telling me to "go find" any toys or treats.
Crawl	This is an easy trick and pretty easy to teach me. Tell me to "lie down". Then place one hand over my shoulders, just touching me. Only place more pressure on my shoulders if I start to get up. Then get a treat in your other hand and wave it under my nose and keep it close to the ground. You can drop the treat just a few inches in front of me. Encourage me to get the treat and when I start to inch forward, tell me to "crawl". You can practice this going all the way across the floor.

Dance	You'll need plenty of treats to teach me how to dance. You can start off with me from either the sit, lie down or stand positions. Take my treat and put it just up over my head with room for me to extend my muzzle. Encourage me to get the treat by letting me sniff it and then lifting the treat high over my head. Give me the treat as soon as I reach it, and tell me to "dance". Practice this until I get the hang of it. Then you can advance to having me "dance" in a circle, just by moving the treat with your hand.

Play Dead	To start this trick, tell me to "lie down" Kneel in front of me. Place a treat in one hand, and let me sniff it. Keep your hand and the treat low to the ground. You'll need your other hand to gently roll my body and head to the ground, and at the same time you'll move the hand with the treat up and over my face, letting me follow it with my head and eyes. Hold my shoulder to the ground and tell me to "play dead". This is all done in one swift motion. Practice and praise me well when I have done good.

As you can see, my obedience commands play an important role in the fun and games that we play.

I'm sure you'll be able to come up with other games or tricks to teach me too.

Missing Vowels

The following words are all found in the Fun and Games section of your book. These words are missing the vowels. Can you fill in the missing vowels to make the words complete?

Use these vowels   A – E – I – O – U – Y

T _ _

C R _ W L

T R _ _ T

G _   F _ N D

B _ G G _ N G

J _ M P

F _ T C H

H _ _ P

P _ W S

S H _ K _

R _ L L

F _ N   G _ M _ S

F _ N D

P L _ _

Unscramble These Words

These words can all be found in the Fun and Games section of your book.

OOPH

BGGGEIN

SHKAE NSHAD

JPMU

PAISER

ENAGECOUR

TTEAR

CHTAE

LLOR EROV

LCRAW

ENADC

FHETC

OG DFIN

OEDBNCIEE

GAESM

TYO

Happy Birthday Card

Birthdays are fun. The next 2 pages have a Happy Birthday card for you to color and send to someone special.

Tear the page carefully out of your book. Once you fold your card on the dotted line, you can write the Happy Birthday greeting on the inside of your card.

To make the card a one-of-a-kind, you could draw some balloons, a cake, some candles or even your favorite type of dog. Then color the pictures in bright colors.

Wishing You A Paw Licking....And A Balloon Popping...

--- Fold Here ----

Draw Me A Tail

More Dog Books

Ask for these other dog books from your favorite bookseller.

Make Your Own Dog Treats   ISBN: 978-1477518755

Traveling Pets   ISBN: 978-1468147452

Dogs, Flags and Their Countries of Origin   ISBN: 978-1466497238

Plus over 100 different dog breed specific books in the "I Want A Pet..." series.

Each dog breed book is a fun learning activity book.

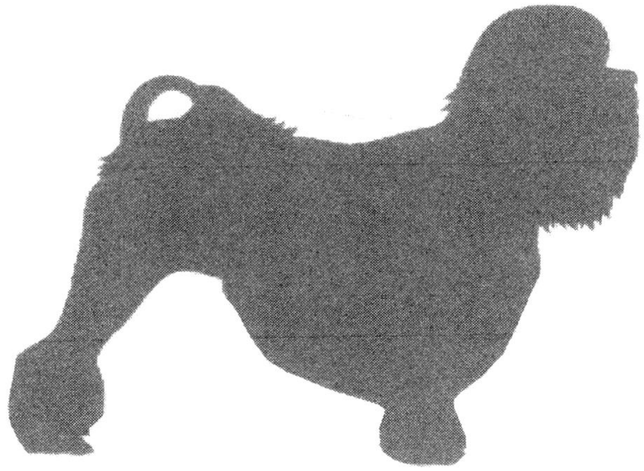

Printed in Great Britain
by Amazon